The G
Samaritan

KEVIN MAYHEW LTD
Rattlesden Bury St Edmunds
Suffolk England
IP30 0SZ

Lutheran Publishing House
205 Halifax Street
Adelaide
SA 5000
Australia

ISBN 0 86209 363 5

Printed in Great Britain

The Good Samaritan

Retold from Scripture by Kathy Singleton
and illustrated by Arthur Baker

Kevin Mayhew

This is a story that Jesus told:

Once upon a time, there was a Jewish trader called Abie. He lived in Jerusalem but his work often took him to far away places. One day Abie decided to visit the markets of Jericho. So, he loaded his donkey with rich materials, he packed some clothes and food and kissed his family good-bye.

It was a long way to Jericho, and
Abie had to walk all the way. The
dusty road led up into the hills, and
wound steeply down on the other
side towards Jericho.

There were huge rocks on either
side of the twisting, turning road
and guess who had hidden behind
those big boulders . . . ?

Bands of nasty robbers! They lay in wait for any travellers who passed by, knives at the ready and eyes glinting greedily.

Abie didn't know what was in store for him. He trudged wearily to the top of the hill. 'Phew, its hot,' he muttered as he mopped his brow.

Suddenly, the robbers pounced! Abie fought back bravely but he was outnumbered. He was knocked to the ground, his money and clothes were stolen, and they even took his donkey! He was left lying in the dust and the robbers disappeared into the hills.

Poor Abie groaned. He couldn't move at all. He just lay there, waiting and hoping that someone would come along.

11

After a while, he heard footsteps.
A Jewish priest appeared. 'Surely
he will help me,' thought Abie.

'Tut, tut!' muttered the priest,
'what a mess! I'll pretend I haven't
seen.' So the priest walked by on
the other side of the road.

A little later, a Levite hurried by, panting heavily. He was due to help the priest at the Synagogue and he was late. 'Oh dear, oh dear,' he mumbled when he saw Abie. 'I can't stop or I'll be late . . . oh dearie me.'

And off he went, leaving poor Abie
lying in the dust.

The sun beat down on Abie. His throat was dry and still he couldn't move.

But what was that he could hear . . . ?
Clip-clop, clip-clop, clip-clop . . .
It was a donkey carrying a Samaritan, called Saul. Abie's heart sank . . . the Jews and the Samaritans were enemies. They just didn't get on at all. 'He won't stop,' Abie thought. But Saul was different . . .

When he saw Abie Saul felt sorry
for him and got down off his
donkey. He reached for his water
bottle and, gently lifting Abie's
head, gave him some water to
drink. 'Thank you,' gasped Abie
weakly. Then Saul bathed Abie's
wounds and tore up his own coat
to make bandages for the
wounded man.

He lifted him gently on to the back of his donkey. Poor Abie was too weak to stay sitting on the donkey and he leant heavily on Saul. But Saul didn't mind. He was glad to help. He walked slowly next to the donkey, as they picked their way down the hillside and into the town of Jericho.

Saul took Abie to the inn where he was staying and put him to bed. All through the night he looked after Abie, wiping his brow, dressing his wounds, and helping him to sip a little water. And, slowly, very slowly, Abie began to get stronger.

The next morning Saul had to leave Jericho but Abie was not well enough to return to Jerusalem. So Saul said to the Inn Keeper: 'Abie has no money but I'll pay for him until he is better. Take good care of him.' He gave the man two silver coins.

Then he mounted his donkey
waved good-bye to Abie and set
off out of Jericho.

'So you see,' Jesus said to the crowd who were listening to him, 'this story shows that we should be kind to everyone, no matter who they are, whether we know them or not, or whether we like them or not.'

Note for parents:
This story can be found in the Gospel according to Luke, chapter 10, verses 29-37.